Build Your Own Brain:

A Roadmap

Greg Farnum

Contents

Section One:
Cars That Watch Us

How We Got There

It's a well planned road,
entrances and exits and signage
all scientifically planned, it leads
right to the center of your mind
—gets you there faster than ever
and when it leaves you off...
you look around and try to remember
what was there before.
It was a marsh.
It was a field.
What was it?

How Will We Know?

The trees across the street
motionless in time (?)
keep watch. What
are they waiting for?
And why?
And what happens
when they find it?

A Place for Man

Wind chimes on a cold winter day
like a chemistry experiment, fascinating in its way
but with an implied warning for humans:
Stay away...stay away...

A Place for Cars

Cat sits at the window
and watches the rain.
And the cars, always cars..

Our Motorized Friends

What did they do to my winter morning,
did they set off a bomb or someting?
Nothing lives out there
except a few cars.

Shop

Must I?
shop carefully
read the small print

                   shop till I drop
            give back to my community

drink responsibly

                   support small business
give thanks for friends and family

give thanks for the car companies
that give thanks for our friends and family.

Give thanks for the car companies again.

The Smart Thing

SHOP SMART

SHOP SMART
SAVE BIG

SHOP BIG
SAVE SMART

SHOP SHOP

BIG SMART

SHOP SHOP
SHOP SHOP

SHOP

Easy Livin'

It had a new, EasyPour top, designed to help me Pour…Easy. It took me awhile to work around it so I could easily pour.

The Good Life

Let's kill things
for trophies;
it's healthy outdoor fun.

Now I Know I'm Safe

Please humiliate me
    so I'll be safer on an airplane
though I never fly

(the fight against terrorism
occurs on many fronts).

Sending a Message

Fishing off the broken highway
all cracked slabs of concrete piled up
at the water's edge
and the spray paint on the largest one says
MAN WAS HERE.

Heart of Stone

Those stones are from the palace,
those over there are from the prison.
They look the same but they're not,
they were dug from the same quarry
and they look the same,
but they're not.
A scrap of paper
tumbles and stops on the sidewalk outside
commenting on the thought.

Harken to the Good News

Good news for America:
We've killed somebody.
It was a bad guy
—we only kill bad guys.
(I know, this poem is too simplistic,
too simplistic to be considered seriously)

bad guys…

That's Me*

The life that gleams off the rear window
of the SUV as the mid-morning sun
catches it.

*Until I Can Get a Better Job

Do I Need One?

Yes, I need a gadget,
any gadget will do
(I've fallen so far behind
— got to start somewhere.)

Changing Trees

The trees have changed their clothes.
Just since I've been sitting here
they've gone from lighthearted to serious
— a somber mien to greet the encroaching evening..
And then a breeze rides in on a burst of sun
and the trees, happy again,
cast off their respectability, wave and shout
"Oh what the hell — after all, I'm a tree!"

Invitation to the Dance

...why do we dance?
Americans dance for products and
fast food treats.
Gimme more gimme more.
Act now call today be you.
You you you you you...
you dance.

Song Lyric (Don't Miss Act Today)

call now

call now

call now

The Logic of an Empty Street

Windy fragments of the day
stabbing the grey air
and stirring up memories
like a spoon in a bowl of soup,
but memories morph into mysteries —
like what was Scarlett Johansson doing in my dream?
As it rounds the corner
a white car beeps at the empty street
obeying its own logic.

(May Lead to Death)

Invitation to the Dance II

dance / buy
buy / dance
product
bonanza
product bonanza
giant BOGO
America morphs into Gomer Pyle
across all devices
more data
more product
more product data
more dancing
more
more
    but I don't mean to preach.

Boldness of Morning

Already the tips of the rosebush
are tinged with autumn;
long, wild and scraggly
they wave in the breeze
daring winter to show its face.

The Victors

We're winning!
The war, the struggle, the contest,
it matters little: we're crushing the competition.
Stick your fist in the air and shout
We're winning!
Isn't that what it's all about?

The Sound of Safety

The garbage truck in my kitchen
makes a beeping sound
just like the microwave
in the parking lot. It's for safety
while the microwave is backing up.

Like a Thing Unknown

Like a formal acknowledgment of personal fault or error
Like a binding or thickening agent used in cooking
Like relating to, involving, or dealing with abstract, general, or universal   statements or laws
Like being unruly or disorderly
Like something tremendous in size, volume, or degree
Like the means or resources for purchasing or doing something
Like gathering or piling in a heap
Like an acutely painful or embarrassing misunderstanding
Like acting as a detective
Like a special magnetic charm or appeal
Like growing or causing to grow by rapid production of new parts, cells, buds, or offspring
Like being in a state of confusion
Like liberal giving (as of money) to or as if to an inferior
Like giving an omen or anticipatory sign
Like the state of being old
Like regarding or treating (something bad or <u>blameworthy</u>) as acceptable, forgivable, or harmless
Like a reasoned train of thought
Like being full of vigor and stamina
Like a thing difficult to comprehend
Like the process of exact thinking
Like withdrawing one's attention
Like being extremely or excessively <u>particular</u>, <u>exacting</u>, or <u>meticulous</u> in taste or standards
Like a harsh or discordant sound
Like the perfect form or example of something
Like the deepest emotions or affections

Like giving expression to <u>emotion</u>
<u>Like being</u> marked by or exhibiting a fawning attentiveness
Like being brought close together
Like an excited commotion
Like being set apart
Like a piece or fragment of a brittle substance
Like propagandistic language marked by <u>euphemism</u>, <u>circumlocu-</u>
<u>tion</u>, and the inversion of customary meanings
Like a dictionary.

(Interlude) Mangen's group emphasize that the sense of touch in print reading adds an important redundancy to information – a kind of "geometry" to words, and a spatial "thereness" for text. As Piper notes, human beings need a knowledge of where they are in time and space that allows them to return to things and learn from re-examination – what he calls the "technology of recurrence". The importance of recurrence for both young and older readers involves the ability to go back, to check and evaluate one's understanding of a text. The question, then, is what happens to comprehension when our youth skim on a screen whose lack of spatial thereness discourages "looking back."

Travel Warning

Don't go there says the State Department, they caution of crime and "arbitrary arrest" and I wonder where are they talking about, Detroit? Pontiac?

I've been to a place where fungal infections are common.

Deal of the day: Vinturi V1071 Red Wine Aerator Tower Set, or consider the SanDisk Ultra Plus Class 10 MicroSD 6468.

MindManager makes it easy to think, plan & communicate.

Veteran gets military funeral after death.

Ariana Grande does something.

Minimally invasive surgery can also be an option.

the often overlooked / everyday cruelty / that made the world go round — Juggle these parts?

Trash Mountain bathed in misty brightness without a wisp of snow to be seem, as if winter had taken a brief vacation.

PROMO CODE USAVEMORE

Former 12 year old boy has cancer with touching moment.

—With a legendary Power Hour and a sophisticated atmosphere.

Brought to you by the US Department of Marketing Services.

Stop.

I saw the picture of the recently deceased LA newscaster with his perfect smile and his perfect hair and his perfect tie and I kept thinking he doesn't look like a real person. I know it sounds like a cliché I told myself, but he doesn't look like a real person.

Experts say Samsung's folding screen phone is a game changer.

Stop. Before you even think of buying that YANAZAKI Home Tosca Key Rack, check out our prices first.

"You may have a gambling problem," says the voice, followed by a caller who declares "NASCAR isn't what it used to be." At that moment a woman in a worn Snap-on Tools jacket, a hood partially covering her face, and a large plastic bag of bottles and cans enters the party store. The caller explains why NASCAR has fallen from its high estate and the Snap-on woman leaves the store without her bag. She stops at the garbage can next to the door, looks inside, pauses, then picks out a bottle and moves on.

Police say the bodies may have been in the car "for days."

Adolph Hitler is trending.

Hair Loss Mental Health — USA BASED

And above all, more ads please.

(end)

The Latest: SIX-FUNCTION Free Market Moon

"Tears Won't Stop" the article said; another celebrity has died.

Is it here yet?

I guess he led the fight against the growing menace of e-cigarettes. Before he died.

Is it here?

Member of the free market think tank explains the new (after he died),

The Apollo 11 mission still has the power to thrill us the newspaper informs me.

Body positive model slams the haters.

Sweet 'n Salty Steak & Guac Signature Wrap is here.

We were in our last stages of infantry training for Vietnam. The drill sergeant (with surgically implanted fangs?) called us out early, more tired and miserable than usual, into the darkness.

"Look up!" he shouted. There it was, big and shining. "We've just walked on the moon. *Dismissed!*"

THE WORLD'S FIRST SIX-FUNCTION MULTIPRO TAIL-GATE is finally here.

Teethmarks on the sky.

Items along the route: So much, he muttered.

Diet Tips

YOU CAN EAT THIS.

That's all it said, except for the fine print and legalese, and pictures and colors. And the instructions of course: Add butter and water.

Section Two: Chants for the 21st Century

Retractable World

What are the ways in which Alarm.com can protect me?
What is my style profile?
Does it range from elegant silhouettes to cozy knitted styles?
Is that me?
What is the sale that has major brands worried?
Should I learn how empowered celebrity bikini photos are defying ageism?
Or how this phone package is really all about family?
Ford, too, is all about family.
And Chevy.

One big family.
My dog went mega-viral and became a beloved meme. Then she suddenly died laments stricken owner.
My dog was family.

Thank you for calling the all-our-representatives-are-busy helpline.
Read the six warning signs of Lupus.

to unriddle itself, the sensorial, perhaps this is
what memories want. — Hans Tentije.

The e-mail was from Freinds of the Donate Now to Make Your Voice Heard.
What are the seven warning signs of cancer?
What part does 5G play in my portfolio?
A new kind of microwave egg sucker?

Officially Licensed Everything

By participating, you agree to the terms & privacy policy (ckq.io/ 31498) for recurring autodialed marketing messages from 314 Action Fund to the phone number you provide. No consent required to buy. Msg&data rates may apply.

Act Now
CLICK HERE for full activation

(laughing)
(screaming)
(electricity zapping)...the monster movie is about to begin.
Chicken battered ocean fried fresh frozen.
Near naked bachlorette shows her toned butt.
How can I earn 80,000 BONUS POINTS (redeemable in up to $1,000 travel rewards)?
Beer battered maple bacon...
Click here for updates.
Republicans unswayed by evidence.
...or try our FAMILY COMBO for only $29.99.
Google debuts a standalone to-do app
...using Nextgen access technology
...the data of 87 million users. (Misused? Stolen?)
Message and data rates apply.
Twelve warning signs you may be heading for Parkinson's.
Retractable World: America's hottest new gadget medicine app.
Terms, conditions, features, availability, pricing, fees, service and support options subject to change without notice.
Kohler's new toilet takes the restroom experience to a whole new level the newspaper tells me.
We strive to hold back the tears.
They're offering near-peer mentoring using data-driven technology.

CLICK HERE FOR MEGA SAVINGS / FLASH SALE
NEW
NOW
NEXT

We strive to hold back the tears. (You know, as a nation.)

They're talking about what today's savvy consumers are looking for.

Today's savvy consumers are looking for a seamless retail experience.

Some restrictions may apply.

Taco Bell is going old school.

What old school are they going to?

CLICH HERE TO LEARN MORE

An Outdoor TV Will Take Your Backyard Enjoyment to the Next Level.

Jardiance will be with me through every step of my journey.

A rare genital infection may occur.

Eighteen signs you are going to die.

FARO Expands Usage of Hoops Toolkits

It's all about family.

CLICK HERE FOR MEGA SAVINGS / FLASH SALE

"You're not from here are you."

> Betty to David Love in *Teenagers from Outer Space.*

How many billionaires do we need?

A rare digital infection may occur.

Mystery drones cause panic in Midwest, Great Plains

Ape Man Burglaries Terrorize City

Behind and on either side of the attractive celebrity whose body had just been found was a small sign saying

NEW
NOW
NEXT
...the incoherence of the modern digital age, filled with sudden shifts from subject to subject, a roller-coaster ride of emotional highs and lows punctuated with commercials. There is nonstop stimulation. Seldom does anything occupy our attention for more than a few seconds. Nothing has context. Images overwhelm words. We are perpetually confused, but always entertained. We barely remember what we saw or heard a few minutes earlier. This is by design of the elites who manipulate us. —Neal Postman

As the police chief said after officers kill a random man in his backyard, "Tragedies happen."

What BUDSGUNSHOP.COM Tells Us About America

Please be advised that firearms often sell quickly following our emails. We hope you found this message useful.

What's Needed

A new treat from the street vendors: duck grease on a stick.
Do I need it…
or do I need innovative voice solutions?
Do I need a look that's as young as I feel?
Do I need a truck that works as hard as I do?
Do I need to synch my alerts across devices?
Do I need subscriber access to premium content?
Do I need to remember that as racing champion Bobby Unser
said, Success is where preparation and opportunity meet.
Do I need to drive the new XT5 to know I've arrived?
Do I need artisanal chocolate bars?
Do I need to know what celebrity sons Dylan and Paris did at the
Golden Globes?
Do I need to know the 11 major Kardashian moments of 2019?
Do I need to know about the Kate Beckinsale photo that is
strictly NSFW?
Do I need to know more about the celebrity I forgot?
Do I really need to know why Ivanka won't commit?
Do I need to know why Aldi shoppers were furious?
Do I need to know?
Do I need to be the Santa of sports nutrition?
Do I need to BOGO on LED hats?
Do I need to know about the scrappy new comedy horror that's
all bark and no bite?
Do I need to know why Avengers: Endgame made even more
money than anticipated?
Do I need to know more about the Georgia couple who were
terrified when a hacker…
Do I need to give back to my community?

Do I need to give back to the heroes?

Do I really need to dance for products?

How shall I know which products to dance for? Will the commercials tell me?

Do I need to know about the crowd pleasing sleepers with surprise megabucks deals?

Do I need to know which celebs are already rocking this fall's hottest fashion trends?

Do I need to know how Paul Walker cracked open the "90s golden boy" schtick?

Do I need to know what that means?

Do I need to know why unions need to start treating employers as partners and not as adversaries?

Do I need to see how Kate Beckansall (sp?) sizzles in beach getaway?

Do I need to read more about a star I'd never heard of?

Do I need a magical Disney vacation?

Do I need to know more about their Wellness Options?

Do I need a car that's been bred for the American road?

Do I need to drive the XT6 to know that I've arrived?

Do I need, as Ciara suggests, to get my funk on?

Do I need to know about the new ingredient that can add zest to my smoothie?

Do I need to know when that time will come again — the time of the giant BOGO…the doorbuster…the monster Sales Event?

Do I need to go viral?

BE THE HOTSPOT. Do I need to do that?

Do I need to capture the meme-train?

Do I need another chance at a vacation in paradise?

Do I need to begin the conversation?

Do I need to follow my dreams?

Do I need to make a compellingly personal statement with my product choices?

Do I need to act now to lock in a great low rate?

Do I need to SHOP NOW to SAVE BIG?

Do I really need ice-blown kettle-boiled barrel-aged old tyme goodness?

Do I really need every aspect of that product?

That can't be real, right? I misheard…right?

Do I need the 1More Piston Fit E 1009 for only 14 pounds in time for the holidays?

Do I need to know about the new biologic that's good news for my colon?

Do I need to see the throwback bikini photo?

Do I need to see football players dancing?

Do I need to follow my dreams of locking in a great low rate while my shoes say a lot about me? Is that the viral conversation I need to begin?

Do I really need to know if this is *really* my last chance to take advantage of these giant BOGO deals?

Do I need to rethink my approach to customized benefits management?

Do I need gluten-free keto-friendly?

Go to dot com slash BOGO.

Do I need to rethink my approach to BOGO? What does the shopping expert say?

Do I need to warn my readers that some scenes may contain violence or smoking?

Do I need to set a reminder to tell me when the game starts?

Do I need to address my digital device by name?

Do I really need to be all that I can be? In the Marines? With Microsoft?

With the Microsoft Marines?

Do I need to know about the six women who are changing the meat industry?

Do I need an experience of excitement and adventure for the whole family?

Do I need to know more about the feel-good movie of the year?

Do I need to know more about this big land of ours?

Go to .com/BOGO.

Do I need to learn more about the natural laxative with fewer side effects?

Do I need to know more about the urban area that offers a vibrant street art scene, a website with powerful engagement tools, and trendy street vendors selling duck grease on a stick?

Be sure to register and use your card to qualify!

Be sure to download the App!

Do I need to check my phone?

Do I need to consume my own tail?

Yes.

Yes, I need it all…and I will have it.

Time is Running Out

Time is running out (these deals won't last forever) on:

Chicken battered ocean fried fresh frozen.

Near naked bachlorette showing her toned butt.

Earn 80,000 BONUS POINTS (redeemable in up to $1,000 travel rewards)?

Beer battered maple bacon...

Click here for updates.

Google debuts a standalone to-do app

...using Nextgen access technology

...the data of 87 million users. (Misused? Stolen?)

Message and data rates apply.

Kohler's new toilet takes the restroom experience to a whole new level the newspaper tells me.

We strive to hold back the tears.

They're offering near-peer mentoring using data-driven technology.

CLICK HERE FOR MEGA SAVINGS / FLASH SALE

NEW

NOW

NEXT

We strive to hold back the tears. (You know, as a nation.)

They're talking about what today's savvy consumers are looking for.

Today's savvy consumers are looking for a seamless retail experience.

Some restrictions may apply.

Taco Bell is going old school.

What old school are they going to?

CLICH HERE TO LEARN MORE

An Outdoor TV Will Take Your Backyard Enjoyment to the Next Level.

Jardiance will be with me through every step of my journey.

FARO Expands Usage of Hoops Toolkits

It's all about family.

Consult with your doctor.

It's all about giving back.

DRIVE FREE

With Adulumdibab I can keep reaching for my best me.

Must be the approaching storm — the picture is breaking up.

Don't wait to see your doctor.

Vembu Backup for Hyper-V?

Upgrade to a Certified Refurbished.

Sweet follen? Perhaps Web MD can help.

Consult with your doctor before...

Racism and violence have no place in our society declared the violent, racist official in a statement released by his office.

Consult with your doctor before...before doing anything.

Make your holiday bright with ad free holiday music and classic hits.

Can I? Can I dream? Must I consult my doctor first? Must I tweet?

Must I tweet my doctor?

Must I tweet my doctor about the sorry state of the Dallas Cowboys?

INSTALL NOW

INSTALL LATER

Thank you for taking part in our survey [YOUR NAME].

Press one if you value your freedom.

The thin whisp of exhaust

skims the wet black pavement

behind the dusky SUV

and both are soon gone.

I'm sorry I didn't understand your last response.

INSTALL NOW

INSTALL LATER

Don't miss the epic holiday season finale of The Masked Fish.

Call. Call now.

Call for this special limited time offer.

Call if you have fallen and can't get up.

Call if you are frightened of the product that will let you be your best self.

Call if you are trapped at the bottom of a mountain of messages.

Call for help. Call. Call now.

Somewhere in the universe there is someone who will hear you.

Expedition to Earth

Seemingly endless expanses of roads with houses and patches of green artfully placed to keep the roads apart, and on all the roads a steady stream of receiving/transmitting stations move back and forth…

Google debuts a standalone to-do app.

…using Nextgen access technology.

…the data of 87 million users.

Is customer service important to you? Of course it is.

I view us more as an experience company that's powered by data and technology.

Just ask your smart speaker.

Message and data rates apply.

The vaunted Silverdome just a hole in the ground now, dust rising from the ground like smoke in a war movie.

Kohler's new toilet takes the restroom experience to a whole new level.

We strive to hold back the tears.

For freshier, healthier gums and feet.

They're offering near-peer mentoring using data-driven technology.

You can get something for as low as $45 a month!

11%

We all want unlimited data.

A succession of small signs by the road that weren't here last week, each offering,
11%?
Of what.

We strive to hold back the tears.

Next time I'm down this stretch of road I pick up the signs again:

11%

Rebate.

Rebate on what?

Rebate on everything in store.

What store?

They're talking about what today's savvy consumers are looking for.

Today's savvy consumers are looking for a seamless retail experience.

What's new? Tina Fey's musical "Mean Girls," which she adapted from her much-beloved and oft-quoted 2004 high school comedy movie.

Do you want more gig speed? Of course you do. We all do. So why are you still…on a highway to hell?

AC/DC is on a Highway to Hell.

—market based, market driven.

Have you heard the good news about Cologard?

Some parents didn't want to get their children vaccinated because they feared it would encourage promiscuity.

Some people are seeking closure.

Yes, we all want more gig speed.
New hope for abandoned mall?

AC/DC is on a Highway to Hell.

Surround yourself with the things that are worthy of your reputation.

Is this the death of retail?

The road is filling up with big vehicles…

Surround yourself…

…bigger vehicles…

…can they possibly get any *bigger* vehicles?

Surround yourself.

It's a crowded road, there's little room for the likes of me –
maybe I should pull over.

The motorized covered wagons with the digital entertainment
systems are rolling – savages beware!

OPENING SOON! said the roadside sign in front of the half built
superstore. OPENING SOON APPLY NOW for more jobs you
can't make a living at.

Cadillacs are besieging the parking lot. They are important – they
have things to do…like go to the other end of the parking lot.

"Unleash the Devil Ray!"

The sacred memory of the incredible Americans who—

"Unleash the Devil Ray!" Soak up the savings during the sum-
mer sales event.

The Aaro family of companies – offering janitorial services and
much more.

Remember the sacred memory.

"Unleash the Devil Ray!" says the Emperor Ming in my mind for some reason. Forget your mind, keep your attention on the road – on the road and your digital entertainment system. Your mind has no place on this road

Section Three: Closed Rooms and Faster Service

NEW OWNERS
    WIDE SELECTION

GREAT DEALS
    LOW PRICES

ALL CAPS
    EVERY DAY

What?
What is the gutter cleaning trick the pros don't want
seniors like me to know?
What? What?
A man rattling the bars yelling *What?*
Which side of the bars is the man on?
Which? What are the ways that I can profit
from the coming 5G boom?
Put a tennis ball in it?
Is that the trick the pros don't want me to know?

at, of, in, to, from, and by

Whereto

to

        to
        to
        to

                to…

to the place

to the place we are heading
to   of

            about…toward…near

to

                near to that place

that place which, to

to
to

to

[to the words that go between the words?]

The game is getting exciting but night is falling.
Go outside and see the sunset.
The game might go into extra innings but the daylight won't.

Elegy for a Whale

Dead whale had ingested 64 pounds of trash
had whale of trash 64 pounds ingested dead
ingested dead trash 64 pounds had whale of
64 pounds whale had of ingested dead trash
of 64 pounds whale had ingested dead trash
ingested trash of 64 pounds dead had whale
trash of ingested had whale dead 64 pounds
had whale 64 pounds trash of ingested dead
of dead ingested had whale 64 pounds trash

Portrait

1
Portrait: Pushhing the baby carriage, he stares at his phone.

But I simplify.

2
I simplify
there's more to him than that

of course there's more to him than that…

3
But at this moment,
at this point in time….

maybe not.

In the Closed Room

Vacant screen

The old typewriter searches
for a clean sheet of paper

what name
will sign the sheet?

Another Helping?

more

more

more

more

more

more

more

more

more

more

more

more

more

more

more

more

more

more

more

more

more

more

stuff

Users

Terrified users
beg security company
to stop hackers.

Fugitives

Single bird alights on the high bare branch
across the street

did the cat notice
through the glass?

cat moves off
so does the bird.

Fugitive sun tries to flash
across the wind chimes
and fails.

The barest hint of clouds
press through the grey sky.
A robin alights on our lawn.